The Road to
Clear Skin

Less Stress & Big Checks

Printed in the USA by A2Z Books, LLC.
Copyright by Natalia President
of Natalia's Magic Skincare
All rights reserved.

This book or any portion thereof may not be reproduced or used in any manner whatsoever without the express written permission of the publisher except for the use of brief quotations in book review Printed in the United States.

First Printing
ISBN 978-1-955148-02-3
www.A2ZBookspublishing.net

Every woman wants Clear Skin, Less Stress and Big Checks.
So I'm taking you through a 30 Day Journey to obtain all 3.
Hi I'm Natalia President CEO of Natalia's Magic Skincare & Royalty Hustle.
I'm going to give you some daily tips and routines to assist you with having clear skin, a more stress free life,
and more financial blessings.
30 Days to Clear Skin, 30 Days to Less Stress, and 30 Days to Big Checks and you can repeat these as needed.

God Is Within Her She Can Not Fall. *Psalm 46:5*

Natalia President

This *Clear Skin, Less Stress, & Big Checks Journal*

Belongs to:

_____

_____

Every girls dream is to have clear skin,

less stress, & big checks.

Natalia President

Clear Skin Assessment

1. How comfortable are you with your skin?

2. What is your current skin care regimen?

3. What is your skin care goal?

Less Stress Assessment

What is your current stress level? _____

1 - Not Stressed at all
2 - Sometimes Stressed
3 - Often Stressed
4 - Always Stressed

What are the things that cause you stress?

What can you do to eliminate stress?

What are my stress level goals? _____

1 - Not Stressed at all
2 - Sometimes Stressed
3 - Often Stressed
4 - Always Stressed

Big Checks Assessment

1. Where am I in my professional life?

2. What is my current financial situation?

3. What are my current financial goals?

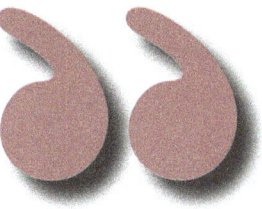

My mission in life is not merely to survive, but to thrive; and to do so with some passion, some compassion, some humor, and some style.

Maya Angelou

Clear Skin, Less Stress, & Big Checks Master List

Clear Skin List:

- Double Cleanse
- Exfoliate
- Tone
- Spot Treat (face mask, serums, or anything to target a specific
- skin need: dark spots, acne, etc.)
- Apply Eye Cream
- Apply Moisturizer / and SPF Moisturizer in the Morning

Less Stress List:

- Take a walk
- Exercise
- Take a nap
- Drink a cup of hot tea
- Meditate
- Do Yoga
- Declutter a room or drawer in your hou[se]
- Listen to music
- Say a Gratitude Affirmation
- Journal

Big Checks 30 Day Savings Challenge.

Saving money is important because it helps reduce financial restraints, assist with small and large purposes and is overall good for your financial health, which is needed to obtain wealth. Over the next 30 Days we will conduct the Big Checks Envelope Savings Challenge that will show you how saving just a little everyday ca[n] add up and help you to reach your financial goals. (See Envelopes)

Clearskin, Less Stress, & Big Checks

```
H E V A S K H A K T E A M I E S T N Y M S I O
P Y E N O M C B Z Z H V Z A Z H G O G I N J S
Y M E X O P L D F N A O O Q O O G U U K F E K
H K R S S E R T S S S E L E S N A E L C N P D
S F I P N G L J F R F R H G F E C Z A X F G X
A Y A P T M I L K Z R A T Q V Y M E G M D G F
C N N A R E S E K B N W R Z V A C N O O T O E
C C O V K J L E M G C Z Y V Y G J G Y O U J T
S T I O M O C L F C O P E Z I R U T S I O M A
W V L O A V N W V W S K C E H C G I B E X Q I
M M L E E R B Z U G E H E W D K L A W V E J L
L B I R R G W N Y Y H A H U A D N D W F P G O
Y A M B C N K E R U D A L E Y T U M W Q G Y F
Z Q Y S E V O L Q F I F Z T B V E E K P Z M X
X M S J Y N C X T Y X K Z G H I R R Y L Q C E
E O C L E A R S K I N K Y E Z N B T E N O T T
```

Find the following words in the puzzle.
Words are hidden ↑ ↓ → ← and ↘ .

BIGCHECKS
CASH
CLEANSE
CLEARSKIN
EXFOLIATE
EYECREAM
HONEY

LESSSTRESS
LOVE
MILK
MILLIONAIRE
MOISTURIZE
MONEY
SAVE

TONE
WALK
WATER
WEALTH
YOGA
ZEN

Day 1 - *The Road to Clear Skin, Less Stress, & Big Checks*

Morning Skin Routine #1 (*Check when completed.*)

- ○ Double cleanse
- ○ Exfoliate
- ○ Moisturize with spf

Less Stress

Choose 2 Things to do from the the Less Stress Master List.

1. _____

2. _____

Big Checks

Grab Envelope #1 and Add $1 to it and put away.

Night time Skin Routine #1 (*Check when completed.*)

- ○ Double cleanse
- ○ Face mask
- ○ Moisturize with spf

Day 1 - *Reflection*

Write how you felt about today?

(If it was bad rip it out and burn)

Today was good because:

Today was bad because:

The Road to Clear Skin
Less Stress & Big Checks

Money Saving Tip:

When you can use cash. Debit and credit card purchases are easy to use, but will have you buying things you don't need because it's so convenient.

Day 2 - *The Road to Clear Skin, Less Stress, & Big Checks*

Morning Skin Routine #2 (*Check when completed.*)

- ○ Double cleanse
- ○ Moisturize with spf

Less Stress

Choose 2 Things to do from the the Less Stress Master List.

1. _____

2. _____

Big Checks

Grab Envelope #2 and Add $2 to it and put away.

Night time Skin Routine #2 (*Check when completed.*)

- ○ Double cleanse
- ○ Moisturize

Day 2- *Reflection*

Write how you felt about today?

(If it was bad rip it out and burn)

Today was good because:

Today was bad because:

The Road to Clear Skin
Less Stress & Big Checks

Motivational Coloring Page

(Coloring assist with relaxation.)

The Road to Clear Skin

Less Stress & Big Checks

Day 3 - *The Road to Clear Skin, Less Stress, & Big Checks*

Morning Skin Routine #1 (*Check when completed.*)

- ○ Double cleanse
- ○ Exfoliate
- ○ Moisturize with spf

Less Stress

Choose 2 Things to do from the the Less Stress Master List.

1. _____

2. _____

Big Checks

Grab Envelope #3 and Add $3 to it and put away.

Night time Skin Routine #1 (*Check when completed.*)

- ○ Double cleanse
- ○ Face mask
- ○ Moisturize with spf

Day 3- *Reflection*

Write how you felt about today?

(If it was bad rip it out and burn)

Today was good because:

_____
_____
_____
_____
_____
_____
_____
_____

Today was bad because:

_____
_____
_____
_____
_____
_____
_____

The Road to Clear Skin
Less Stress & Big Checks

<u>Less Stress Tip:</u>

Do something to connect with nature.

Day 4 - *The Road to Clear Skin, Less Stress, & Big Checks*

Morning Skin Routine #2 (*Check when completed.*)

- ○ Double cleanse
- ○ Moisturize with spf

Less Stress

Choose 2 Things to do from the the Less Stress Master List.

1. _____

2. _____

Big Checks

Grab Envelope #4 and Add $4 to it and put away.

Night time Skin Routine #2 (*Check when completed.*)

- ○ Double cleanse
- ○ Moisturize

Day 4- Reflection

Write how you felt about Today?

(If it was bad rip it out and burn)

Today was good because:

_____
_____
_____
_____
_____
_____
_____
_____
_____

Today was bad because:

_____
_____
_____
_____
_____
_____
_____
_____

The Road to Clear Skin

Less Stress & Big Checks

Motivational Coloring Page

(Coloring assist with relaxation.)

The Road to Clear Skin

Less Stress & Big Checks

Clear Skin Tip:

Limit your juices, sodas, sweets, and sugar for clear skin.

Day 5 - *The Road to Clear Skin, Less Stress, & Big Checks*

Morning Skin Routine #1 (*Check when completed.*)

- ○ Double cleanse
- ○ Exfoliate
- ○ Moisturize with spf

Less Stress

Choose 2 Things to do from the the Less Stress Master List.

1. _____

2. _____

Big Checks

Grab Envelope #5 and Add $5 to it and put away.

Night time Skin Routine #1 (*Check when completed.*)

- ○ Double cleanse
- ○ Face mask
- ○ Moisturize with spf

Day 5 - *Reflection*

Write how you felt about today?

(If it was bad rip it out and burn)

Today was good because:

_____
_____
_____
_____
_____
_____
_____
_____

Today was bad because:

_____
_____
_____
_____
_____
_____
_____

The Road to Clear Skin
Less Stress & Big Checks

<u>Money Saving Tip:</u>

Always pay yourself first, by saving.

Day 6 - *The Road to Clear Skin, Less Stress, & Big Checks*

Morning Skin Routine #2 (*Check when completed.*)

- ○ Double cleanse
- ○ Moisturize with spf

Less Stress

Choose 2 Things to do from the the Less Stress Master List.

1. _____

2. _____

Big Checks

Grab Envelope #6 and Add $6 to it and put away.

Night time Skin Routine #2 (*Check when completed.*)

- ○ Double cleanse
- ○ Moisturize

Day 6 - *Reflection*

Write how you felt about today?

(If it was bad rip it out and burn)

Today was good because:

_____
_____
_____
_____
_____
_____
_____
_____

Today was bad because:

_____
_____
_____
_____
_____
_____
_____
_____

The Road to Clear Skin
Less Stress & Big Checks

Motivational Coloring Page

(Coloring assist with relaxation.)

The Road to Clear Skin

Less Stress & Big Checks

Less Stress Tip:

Write a love letter to yourself.

Day 7 - *The Road to Clear Skin, Less Stress, & Big Checks*

Morning Skin Routine #1 (*Check when completed.*)

- ○ Double cleanse
- ○ Exfoliate
- ○ Moisturize with spf

Less Stress

Choose 2 Things to do from the the Less Stress Master List.

1. _____

2. _____

Big Checks

Grab Envelope #7 and Add $7 to it and put away.

Night time Skin Routine #1 (*Check when completed.*)

- ○ Double cleanse
- ○ Face mask
- ○ Moisturize with spf

Day 7 - Reflection

Write how you felt about today?

(If it was bad rip it out and burn)

Today was good because:

Today was bad because:

The Road to Clear Skin
Less Stress & Big Checks

Less Stress Tip:

Stay away from people and things that makes you uncomfortable no matter who they are.

Day 8 - *The Road to Clear Skin, Less Stress, & Big Checks*

Morning Skin Routine #2 (*Check when completed.*)

- ○ Double cleanse
- ○ Moisturize with spf

Less Stress

Choose 2 Things to do from the the Less Stress Master List.

1. _____

2. _____

Big Checks

Grab Envelope #8 and Add $8 to it and put away.

Night time Skin Routine #2 (*Check when completed.*)
- ○ Double cleanse
- ○ Moisturize

Day 8 - Reflection

Write how you felt about today?

(If it was bad rip it out and burn)

Today was good because:

Today was bad because:

The Road to Clear Skin
Less Stress & Big Checks

Motivational Coloring Page

(Coloring assist with relaxation.)

The Road to Clear Skin
Less Stress & Big Checks

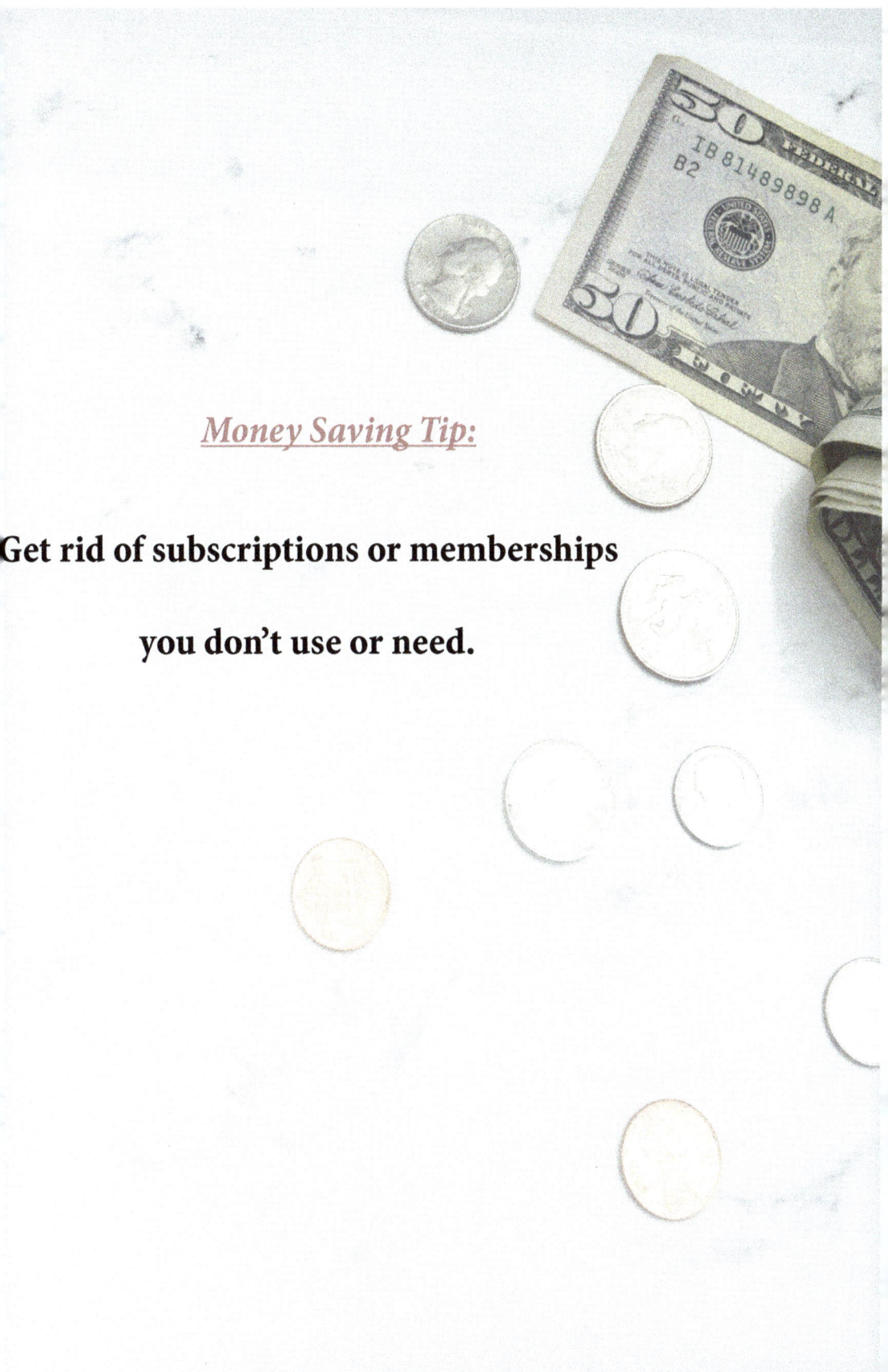

Money Saving Tip:

Get rid of subscriptions or memberships you don't use or need.

Day 9 - *The Road to Clear Skin, Less Stress, & Big Checks*

Morning Skin Routine #1 (*Check when completed.*)

- ○ Double cleanse
- ○ Exfoliate
- ○ Moisturize with spf

Less Stress

Choose 2 Things to do from the the Less Stress Master List.

1. _____

2. _____

Big Checks

Grab Envelope #9 and Add $9 to it and put away.

Night time Skin Routine #1 (*Check when completed.*)

- ○ Double cleanse
- ○ Face mask
- ○ Moisturize with spf

Day 9- Reflection

Write how you felt about today?

(If it was bad rip it out and burn)

Today was good because:

_____
_____
_____
_____
_____
_____
_____
_____
_____

Today was bad because:

_____
_____
_____
_____
_____
_____
_____
_____

The Road to Clear Skin
Less Stress & Big Checks

<u>Clear Skin Tip:</u>

Sleeping on 100% silk or satin pillow cases

will help keep your

skin clear by preventing acne and wrinkles.

Day 10 - *The Road to Clear Skin, Less Stress, & Big Checks*

Morning Skin Routine #2 (*Check when completed.*)

- ○ Double cleanse
- ○ Moisturize with spf

Less Stress

Choose 2 Things to do from the the Less Stress Master List.

1. _____

2. _____

Big Checks

Grab Envelope #10 and Add $10 to it and put away.

Night time Skin Routine #2 (*Check when completed.*)

- ○ Double cleanse
- ○ Moisturize

Day 10-Reflection

Write how you felt about today?

(If it was bad rip it out and burn)

Today was good because:

___

Today was bad because:

The Road to Clear Skin
Less Stress & Big Checks

Motivational Coloring Page

(Coloring assist with relaxation.)

The Road to Clear Skin

Less Stress & Big Checks

Less Stress Tip:

Do what makes you and only you happy.

Day 11 - *The Road to Clear Skin, Less Stress, & Big Checks*

Morning Skin Routine #1 (*Check when completed.*)

- ○ Double cleanse
- ○ Exfoliate
- ○ Moisturize with spf

Less Stress

Choose 2 Things to do from the the Less Stress Master List.

1. _____

2. _____

Big Checks

Grab Envelope #11 and Add $11 to it and put away.

Night time Skin Routine #1 (*Check when completed.*)

- ○ Double cleanse
- ○ Face mask
- ○ Moisturize with spf

Day 11-*Reflection*

Write how you felt about today?

(If it was bad rip it out and burn)

Today was good because:

_____
_____
_____
_____
_____
_____
_____

Today was bad because:

_____
_____
_____
_____
_____

The Road to Clear Skin
Less Stress & Big Checks

Money Saving Tip:

Always keep track of your spending.

Day 12 - *The Road to Clear Skin, Less Stress, & Big Checks*

Morning Skin Routine #2 (*Check when completed.*)

- ○ Double cleanse
- ○ Moisturize with spf

Less Stress

Choose 2 Things to do from the the Less Stress Master List.

1. _____

2. _____

Big Checks

Grab Envelope #12 and Add $12 to it and put away.

Night time Skin Routine #2 (*Check when completed.*)

- ○ Double cleanse
- ○ Moisturize

Day 12-*Reflection*

Write how you felt about Today?

(If it was bad rip it out and burn)

Today was good because:

Today was bad because:

The Road to Clear Skin
Less Stress & Big Checks

Motivational Coloring Page

(Coloring assist with relaxation.)

The Road to Clear Skin
Less Stress & Big Checks

Clear Skin Tip:

Change face cloths daily or use disposable paper cloths

for cleaning skin to help keep skin clear,

because used face cloths are full of bacteria,

which causes acne.

Day 13 - *The Road to Clear Skin, Less Stress, & Big Checks*

Morning Skin Routine #1 (*Check when completed.*)

- ○ Double cleanse
- ○ Exfoliate
- ○ Moisturize with spf

Less Stress

Choose 2 Things to do from the the Less Stress Master List.

1. _____

2. _____

Big Checks

Grab Envelope #13 and Add $13 to it and put away.

Night time Skin Routine #1 (*Check when completed.*)

- ○ Double cleanse
- ○ Face mask
- ○ Moisturize with spf

Day 13-Reflection

Write how you felt about today?

(If it was bad rip it out and burn)

Today was good because:

Today was bad because:

The Road to Clear Skin
Less Stress & Big Checks

Less Stress Tip:

Take a breath.

Day 14 - The Road to Clear Skin, Less Stress, & Big Checks

Morning Skin Routine #2 (*Check when completed.*)

- ○ Double cleanse
- ○ Moisturize with spf

Less Stress

Choose 2 Things to do from the the Less Stress Master List.

1. _____

2. _____

Big Checks

Grab Envelope #14 and Add $14 to it and put away.

Night time Skin Routine #2 (*Check when completed.*)

- ○ Double cleanse
- ○ Moisturize

Day 14-Reflection

Write how you felt about today?

(If it was bad rip it out and burn)

Today was good because:

_____
_____
_____
_____
_____
_____
_____
_____

Today was bad because:

_____
_____
_____
_____
_____
_____
_____

The Road to Clear Skin
Less Stress & Big Checks

Motivational Coloring Page

(Coloring assist with relaxation.)

The Road to Clear Skin
Less Stress & Big Checks

Money Saving Tip:

Decrease your overall debt.

Day 15 - *The Road to Clear Skin, Less Stress, & Big Checks*

Morning Skin Routine #1 (*Check when completed.*)

- ○ Double cleanse
- ○ Exfoliate
- ○ Moisturize with spf

Less Stress

Choose 2 Things to do from the the Less Stress Master List.

1. _____

2. _____

Big Checks

Grab Envelope #15 and Add $15 to it and put away.

Night time Skin Routine #1 (*Check when completed.*)

- ○ Double cleanse
- ○ Face mask
- ○ Moisturize with spf

Day 15-*Reflection*

Write how you felt about Today?

(If it was bad rip it out and burn)

Today was good because:

_____
_____
_____
_____
_____
_____
_____
_____

Today was bad because:

_____
_____
_____
_____
_____
_____
_____
_____

The Road to Clear Skin

Less Stress & Big Checks

Clear Skin Tip:

Turmeric Facemask used for dark spots.

Ingredients:

- 1 tablespoon of Tumeric Powder.
- 2 slices of lemon squeezed for the lemon juice.
- 1 tablespoon of Organic Honey.
- Mix together in a bowl.
- Apply to face gently for 5 to 10 minutes.

Day 16- *The Road to Clear Skin, Less Stress, & Big Checks*

Morning Skin Routine #2 (*Check when completed.*)

- ○ Double cleanse
- ○ Moisturize with spf

Less Stress

Choose 2 Things to do from the the Less Stress Master List.

1. _____

2. _____

Big Checks

Grab Envelope #16 and Add $16 to it and put away.

Night time Skin Routine #2 (*Check when completed.*)

- ○ Double cleanse
- ○ Moisturize

Day 16-Reflection

Write how you felt about today?

(If it was bad rip it out and burn)

Today was good because:

Today was bad because:

The Road to Clear Skin

Less Stress & Big Checks

Motivational Coloring Page

(Coloring assist with relaxation.)

The Road to Clear Skin
Less Stress & Big Checks

Less Stress Tip:

Count from 10 backwards.

Day 17 - *The Road to Clear Skin, Less Stress, & Big Checks*

Morning Skin Routine #1 (*Check when completed.*)

- ○ Double cleanse
- ○ Exfoliate
- ○ Moisturize with spf

Less Stress

Choose 2 Things to do from the the Less Stress Master List.

1. _____

2. _____

Big Checks

Grab Envelope #17 and Add $17 to it and put away.

Night time Skin Routine #1 (*Check when completed.*)

- ○ Double cleanse
- ○ Face mask
- ○ Moisturize with spf

Day 17-Reflection

Write how you felt about Today?

(If it was bad rip it out and burn)

Today was good because:
___

Today was bad because:
___

The Road to Clear Skin
Less Stress & Big Checks

Money Saving Tip:

Make sure you know your needs from your wants.

Day 18 - *The Road to Clear Skin, Less Stress, & Big Checks*

Morning Skin Routine #2 (*Check when completed.*)

○ Double cleanse

○ Moisturize with spf

Less Stress

Choose 2 Things to do from the the Less Stress Master List.

1. _____

2. _____

Big Checks

Grab Envelope #18 and Add $18 to it and put away.

Night time Skin Routine #2 (*Check when completed.*)

○ Double cleanse
○ Moisturize

Day 18-Reflection

Write how you felt about today?

(If it was bad rip it out and burn)

Today was good because:

_____
_____
_____
_____
_____
_____
_____
_____

Today was bad because:

_____
_____
_____
_____
_____
_____
_____

The Road to Clear Skin

Less Stress & Big Checks

Motivational Coloring Page

(Coloring assist with relaxation.)

The Road to Clear Skin

Less Stress & Big Checks

Clear Skin Tip:

For hyperpigmentation and wrinkles, combine turmeric with yogurt and lemon juice for extra nourishment and brightening effects.

Day 19 - *The Road to Clear Skin, Less Stress, & Big Checks*

Morning Skin Routine #1 (*Check when completed.*)

- ○ Double cleanse
- ○ Exfoliate
- ○ Moisturize with spf

Less Stress

Choose 2 Things to do from the the Less Stress Master List.

1. _____

2. _____

Big Checks

Grab Envelope #19 and Add $19 to it and put away.

Night time Skin Routine #1 (*Check when completed.*)

- ○ Double cleanse
- ○ Face mask
- ○ Moisturize with spf

Day 19-Reflection

Write how you felt about today?

(If it was bad rip it out and burn)

Today was good because:

Today was bad because:

The Road to Clear Skin
Less Stress & Big Checks

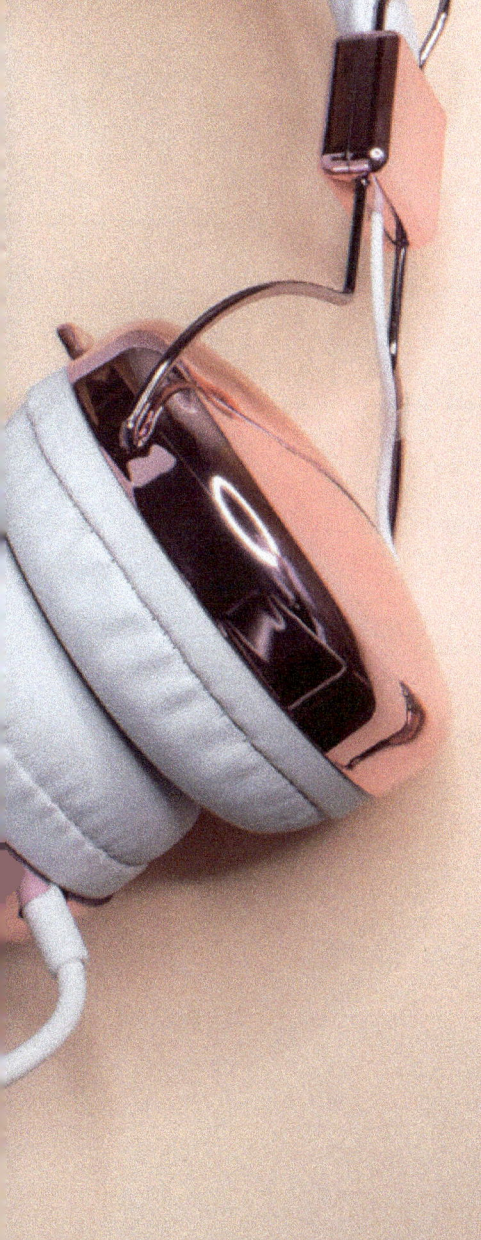

<u>*Less Stress Tip:*</u>

Create a playlist of music that puts you in a good mood.

Day 20 - *The Road to Clear Skin, Less Stress, & Big Checks*

Morning Skin Routine #2 (*Check when completed.*)

- ○ Double cleanse
- ○ Moisturize with spf

Less Stress

Choose 2 Things to do from the the Less Stress Master List.

1. _____

2. _____

Big Checks

Grab Envelope #20 and Add $20 to it and put away.

Night time Skin Routine #2 (*Check when completed.*)

- ○ Double cleanse
- ○ Moisturize

Day 20-Reflection

Write how you felt about today?

(If it was bad rip it out and burn)

Today was good because:

_____
_____
_____
_____
_____
_____
_____
_____

Today was bad because:

_____
_____
_____
_____
_____
_____

The Road to Clear Skin

Less Stress & Big Checks

Motivational Coloring Page

(Coloring assist with relaxation.)

The Road to Clear Skin

Less Stress & Big Checks

Money Saving Tip:

Cook food instead of buying food.

Day 21 - *The Road to Clear Skin, Less Stress, & Big Checks*

Morning Skin Routine #1 (*Check when completed.*)

- ○ Double cleanse
- ○ Exfoliate
- ○ Moisturize with spf

Less Stress

Choose 2 Things to do from the the Less Stress Master List.

1. _____

2. _____

Big Checks

Grab Envelope #21 and Add $21 to it and put away.

Night time Skin Routine #1 (*Check when completed.*)

- ○ Double cleanse
- ○ Face mask
- ○ Moisturize with spf

Day 21-Reflection

Write how you felt about today?

(If it was bad rip it out and burn)

Today was good because:

Today was bad because:

The Road to Clear Skin

Less Stress & Big Checks

Clear Skin Tip:

Honey & Oatmeal Mask for soothing.

Ingredients:

- 2 tablespoons ground oats
- 1 tablespoon of organic honey
- 1 tablespoon hot water
- Mix together in a bowl.
- Gently apply to face and let sit for 10-15 minutes.
- Rinse off with Cold Water.

Day 22 - *The Road to Clear Skin, Less Stress, & Big Checks*

Morning Skin Routine #2 (*Check when completed.*)

- ○ Double cleanse
- ○ Moisturize with spf

Less Stress

Choose 2 Things to do from the the Less Stress Master List.

1. _____

2. _____

Big Checks

Grab Envelope #22 and Add $22 to it and put away.

Night time Skin Routine #2 (*Check when completed.*)

- ○ Double cleanse
- ○ Moisturize

Day 22-Reflection

Write how you felt about today?

(If it was bad rip it out and burn)

Today was good because:

_____
_____
_____
_____
_____
_____
_____
_____

Today was bad because:

_____
_____
_____
_____
_____
_____
_____
_____

The Road to Clear Skin
Less Stress & Big Checks

Motivational Coloring Page

(Coloring assist with relaxation.)

The Road to Clear Skin

Less Stress & Big Checks

Less Stress Tip:

Laugh out loud.

Day 23 - *The Road to Clear Skin, Less Stress, & Big Checks*

Morning Skin Routine #1 (*Check when completed.*)

- ○ Double cleanse
- ○ Exfoliate
- ○ Moisturize with spf

Less Stress

Choose 2 Things to do from the the Less Stress Master List.

1. _____

2. _____

Big Checks

Grab Envelope #23 and Add $23 to it and put away.

Night time Skin Routine #1 (*Check when completed.*)

- ○ Double cleanse
- ○ Face mask
- ○ Moisturize with spf

Day 23-Reflection

Write how you felt about today?

(If it was bad rip it out and burn)

Today was good because:

Today was bad because:

The Road to Clear Skin
Less Stress & Big Checks

Day 24 - *The Road to Clear Skin, Less Stress, & Big Checks*

Morning Skin Routine #2 (*Check when completed.*)

- ○ Double cleanse
- ○ Moisturize with spf

Less Stress

Choose 2 Things to do from the the Less Stress Master List.

1. _____

2. _____

Big Checks

Grab Envelope #24 and Add $24 to it and put away.

Night time Skin Routine #2 (*Check when completed.*)

- ○ Double cleanse
- ○ Moisturize

Day 24-Reflection

Write how you felt about today?

(If it was bad rip it out and burn)

Today was good because:

Today was bad because:

The Road to Clear Skin

Less Stress & Big Checks

Motivational Coloring Page

(Coloring assist with relaxation.)

The Road to Clear Skin

Less Stress & Big Checks

<u>Clear Skin Tip:</u>

Wash your face twice away.

Day 25 - *The Road to Clear Skin, Less Stress, & Big Checks*

Morning Skin Routine #1 (*Check when completed.*)

- ○ Double cleanse
- ○ Exfoliate
- ○ Moisturize with spf

Less Stress

Choose 2 Things to do from the the Less Stress Master List.

1. _____

2. _____

Big Checks

Grab Envelope #25 and Add $25 to it and put away.

Night time Skin Routine #1 (*Check when completed.*)

- ○ Double cleanse
- ○ Face mask
- ○ Moisturize with spf

Day 25-Reflection

Write how you felt about today?

(If it was bad rip it out and burn)

Today was good because:

_____
_____
_____
_____
_____
_____
_____
_____

Today was bad because:

_____
_____
_____
_____
_____
_____
_____
_____

The Road to Clear Skin
Less Stress & Big Checks

Less Stress Tip:

Reduce your caffeine intake.

Day 26 - *The Road to Clear Skin, Less Stress, & Big Checks*

Morning Skin Routine #2 (*Check when completed.*)

- ○ Double cleanse
- ○ Moisturize with spf

Less Stress

Choose 2 Things to do from the the Less Stress Master List.

1. _____

2. _____

Big Checks

Grab Envelope #26 and Add $26 to it and put away.

Night time Skin Routine #2 (*Check when completed.*)

- ○ Double cleanse
- ○ Moisturize

Day 26-Reflection

Write how you felt about today?

(If it was bad rip it out and burn)

Today was good because:

Today was bad because:

The Road to Clear Skin

Less Stress & Big Checks

Motivational Coloring Page

(Coloring assist with relaxation.)

The Road to Clear Skin
Less Stress & Big Checks

Money Saving Tip:

Minimize your credit card usage.

Day 27 - *The Road to Clear Skin, Less Stress, & Big Checks*

Morning Skin Routine #1 (*Check when completed.*)

- ○ Double cleanse
- ○ Exfoliate
- ○ Moisturize with spf

Less Stress

Choose 2 Things to do from the the Less Stress Master List.

1. _____

2. _____

Big Checks

Grab Envelope #27 and Add $27 to it and put away.

Night time Skin Routine #1 (*Check when completed.*)

- ○ Double cleanse
- ○ Face mask
- ○ Moisturize with spf

Day 27-Reflection

Write how you felt about today?

(If it was bad rip it out and burn)

Today was good because:

Today was bad because:

The Road to Clear Skin
Less Stress & Big Checks

<u>*Clear Skin Tip:*</u>

Stay away from dairy(milk, cheese, butter etc.)

because it increases your

oil production which causes blocked pores

and causes acne.

Day 28 - *The Road to Clear Skin, Less Stress, & Big Checks*

Morning Skin Routine #2 (*Check when completed.*)

- ○ Double cleanse
- ○ Moisturize with spf

Less Stress

Choose 2 Things to do from the the Less Stress Master List.

1. _____

2. _____

Big Checks

Grab Envelope #28 and Add $28 to it and put away.

Night time Skin Routine #2 (*Check when completed.*)

- ○ Double cleanse
- ○ Moisturize

Day 28-Reflection

Write how you felt about Today?

(If it was bad rip it out and burn)

Today was good because:

_____
_____
_____
_____
_____
_____
_____
_____
_____

Today was bad because:

_____
_____
_____
_____
_____
_____
_____

The Road to Clear Skin
Less Stress & Big Checks

Less Stress Tip:

Create a spot in your house that makes you very comfortable.

Day 29 - *The Road to Clear Skin, Less Stress, & Big Checks*

Morning Skin Routine #1 (*Check when completed.*)

- ◯ Double cleanse
- ◯ Exfoliate
- ◯ Moisturize with spf

Less Stress

Choose 2 Things to do from the the Less Stress Master List.

1. _____

2. _____

Big Checks

Grab Envelope #29 and Add $29 to it and put away.

Night time Skin Routine #1 (*Check when completed.*)

- ◯ Double cleanse
- ◯ Face mask
- ◯ Moisturize with spf

Day 29-*Reflection*

Write how you felt about today?

(If it was bad rip it out and burn)

Today was good because:

Today was bad because:

The Road to Clear Skin
Less Stress & Big Checks

Money Saving Tip:

Cut down on your grocery bill by creating a grocery list and only buying what you need at that time.

Day 30 - *The Road to Clear Skin, Less Stress, & Big Checks*

Morning Skin Routine #2 (*Check when completed.*)

- ◯ Double cleanse
- ◯ Moisturize with spf

Less Stress

Choose 2 Things to do from the the Less Stress Master List.

1. _____

2. _____

Big Checks

Grab Envelope #30 and Add $30 to it and put away.

Night time Skin Routine #2 (*Check when completed.*)

- ◯ Double cleanse
- ◯ Moisturize

Day 30-*Reflection*

Write how you felt about Today?

(If it was bad rip it out and burn)

Today was good because:

Today was bad because:

The Road to Clear Skin
Less Stress & Big Checks

Motivational Coloring Page

(Coloring assist with relaxation.)

The Road to Clear Skin

Less Stress & Big Checks

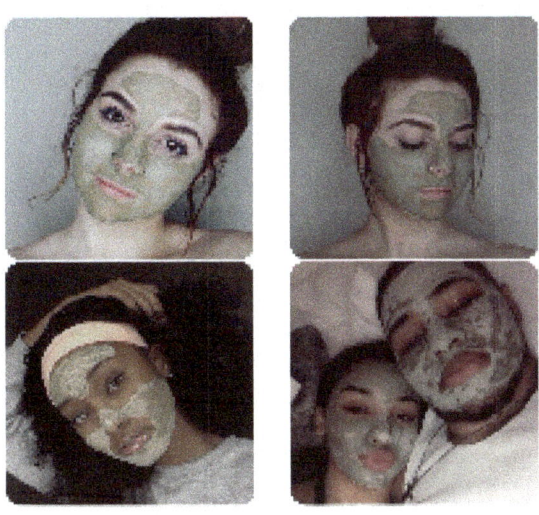

Clear Skin Tip:

Got Pimples? Use the Green tea Detox Face Mask.

available at www.nataliasmagicskincare.com

Congratulations you've completed the
Road to Clear Skin, Less Stress & Big Checks 30 Day Journal.

Feel free to repeat the days & steps to continue on your Clear Skin, Less Stress, & Big Checks Journey.

Visit: www.nataliasmagicskincare.com
for more resources and products.

Interested in Writing & Publishing your own
Book or Journal?
Contact Dr. Synovia on Instagram and
@www.a2zbookspublishing.net

www.ingramcontent.com/pod-product-compliance
Lightning Source LLC
Chambersburg PA
CBHW061203070526
44579CB00010B/117